bebop classics

Arranged by Brent Edstrom

contents

ISBN 978-1-4950-9471-2

HAL•LEONARD®

7777 W. BLUEMOUND RD. P.O. BOX 13819 MILWAUKEE, WI 53213

Visit Hal Leonard Online at
www.halleonard.com

BE-BOP

By JOHN "DIZZY" GILLESPIE

BLUE BREW

By BREW MOORE

Arrangement based on one by Brew Moore

BONEOLOGY

By J.J. JOHNSON

Solo based on one by J. J. Johnson

BOHEMIA AFTER DARK

By OSCAR PETTIFORD

Solo based on one by Horace Silver

CATTIN'

Medium Swing

Arrangement based on one by John Coltrane

Solo based on one by Mal Waldron

DISORDER AT THE BORDER

By COLEMAN HAWKINS

24

LAIRD BAIRD

By CHARLIE PARKER

ECLYPSO

By TOMMY FLANAGAN

Moderate Latin groove

Arrangement based on one by Tommy Flanagan

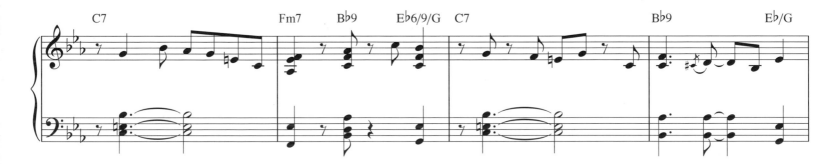

52ND STREET THEME

By THELONIOUS MONK

Solo based on one by Don Byas

34

FOUR BROTHERS

By JIMMY GIUFFRE

GOIN' TO MINTON'S

By THEODORE "FATS" NAVARRO

Fast Swing

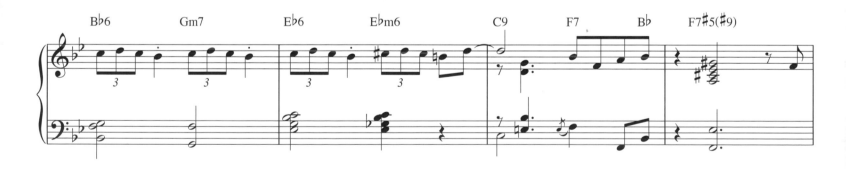

GRAND CENTRAL

By JOHN COLTRANE

To Coda

Solo based on one by Wynton Kelly

HALLUCINATIONS

By EARL "BUD" POWELL

Arrangement based on one by Bud Powell

JAY BIRD

By J.J. JOHNSON

Arrangement based on one by J. J. Johnson

LENNIE'S PENNIES

By LENNIE TRISTANO

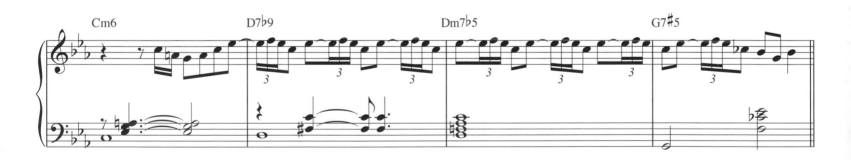

LESTER LEAPS IN

By LESTER YOUNG

Solo based on one by Lester Young

62

OW

By DIZZY GILLESPIE

PARISIAN THOROUGHFARE

By EARL "BUD" POWELL

Arrangement based on one by Bud Powell

PROFESSOR BOP

By BOB GONZALES

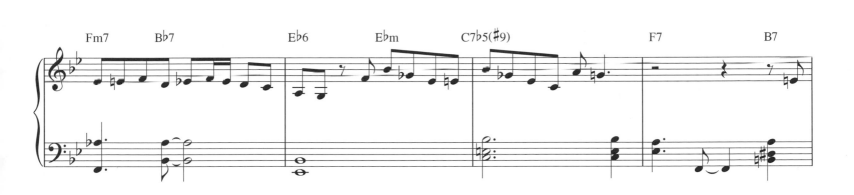

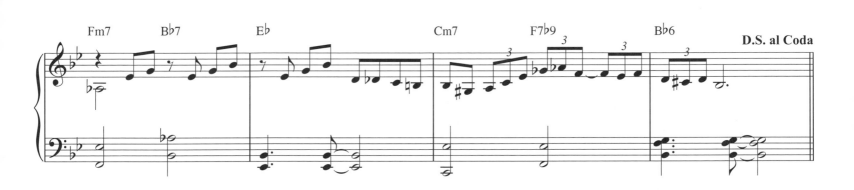

SECOND BALCONY JUMP

By BILLY ECKSTINE
and GERALD VALENTINE

Solo based on one by Dexter Gordon

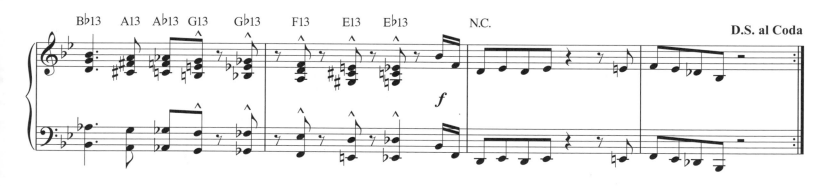

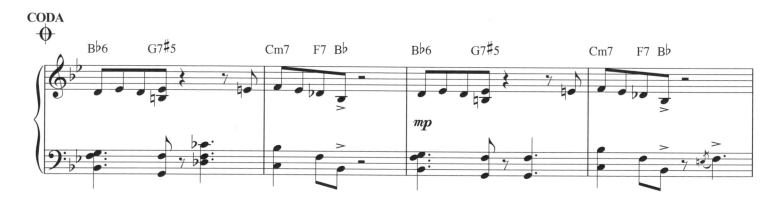

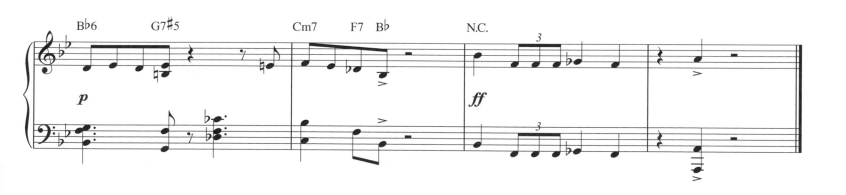

THE SERPENT'S TOOTH

By MILES DAVIS

Solo based on one by Walter Bishop Jr.

STEEPLECHASE

By CHARLIE PARKER

Solo based on one by Charlie Parker

WITCHES PIT

By PEPPER ADAMS

Bright Swing

Arrangement based on one by John Coltrane

MOVE

By DENZIL DE COSTA BEST

Solo based on one by Stan Getz

94